Made in United States
Cleveland, OH
07 January 2025

13159070R00065